Then & Now

Samantha Berger • Daniel Moreton

Scholastic Inc.
New York • Toronto • London • Auckland • Sydney

Acknowledgments

Early Childhood Consultant: Ellen Booth Church

Literacy Specialist: Linda Cornwell

Design: Silver Editions

Photo Research: Silver Editions

Endnotes: Susan Russell

Endnote Illustrations: Ruth Flanigan

———————————————

Photographs: Cover: (l) Bruce Hands/Tony Stone Images; (r) Andy Sacks/Tony Stone Images; p. 1: (l) Jeff Greenberg/Photo Researchers, Inc.; (r) B. Daemmrich/The Image Works; p. 2: Tom Burnside/Photo Researchers, Inc.; p. 3: David Young-Wolff/Photo Edit; p. 4: Harvey Lloyd/The Stock Market; p. 5: David Lawrence/The Stock Market; p. 6: Tony Freeman/Photo Edit; p. 7: Bob Thomas/Tony Stone Images; p. 8: Bruce Hands/Tony Stone Images; p. 9: Andy Sacks/Tony Stone Images; p. 10: Brooks/Brown/Photo Researchers, Inc.; p. 11: Esbin-Anderson/The Image Works; p. 12: (l) Robert Ginn/Photo Edit; (r) Tony Freeman/Photo Edit.

16 15 14 13 12 11   08   8 9 10 11 12 / 0

Then and now.

This is a car from long ago.

Look at cars now.

This is a plane from long ago.

Look at planes now.

This is a camera from long ago.

Look at cameras now.

This is a tractor from long ago.

Look at tractors now.

This is a telephone from long ago.

Look at telephones now.

Things change!

Then & Now

Stoves Some inventions change little by little as technology advances. The stove on the left looked very modern in the late 1800s. It used wood for fuel and provided heat for the house as well as a place for cooking. The stove on the right looks familiar to us now. The stoves we use today, like this one, are powered by natural gas or by electricity. Some stoves are even powered by microwaves!

Cars One of the first automobiles in the United States was created by Henry Ford about a hundred years ago. When he first drove it in the streets of Detroit, its loud engine frightened the horses that pulled the carriages! It was not a popular invention at first. But people needed faster transportation for long distances, and soon they realized the usefulness of the car. Over time, the automobile developed from the Model T of 1914, to the Volkswagen, which is familiar to us today. Each year, many small changes have been made to improve cars—everything from fuel to tires to kinds of paint. The automobile does its job much better now than it did a hundred years ago. It goes faster and provides a smoother ride.

Cameras Cameras were originally invented in the mid-1800s. They were very bulky and used large plates coated with chemicals as film. Whatever was being photographed had to remain still in front of the camera for a long time. Many inventors from around the world improved the technology of photography. By the 1930s, cameras like the one on the left were small and portable. People could photograph their friends wherever they were. These pictures became known as snapshots. They were all black and white. Today many other technological changes have made the camera very easy to use. We have cameras that focus their lenses automatically and give us snapshots with beautiful colors!

Planes The technology for making flying machines came about only at the turn of the century. Two brothers named Orville and Wilbur Wright invented a small engine and propeller that could lift their airplane into the air. The first successful flight was made in North Carolina in 1903 after

many practice trials. The airplane on the left is a much-improved version from the 1920s. Many inventors have applied scientific discoveries from physics and chemistry to create the jet-powered planes that we have today. The modern jet is far bigger and more powerful than the first airplane. It can carry hundreds of passengers and lots of cargo.

Tractors When people started planting and growing food many thousands of years ago, they needed to turn over the soil to make it soft and ready for the seeds, a method known as plowing. First, the plow was invented, an instrument for digging into the earth. People pushed the plow to make it move. Later, a plow was invented that could be pulled by animals like horses or oxen. The picture on the left shows a horse-drawn plow. When gasoline engines were invented at the turn of the century, they were used not only for cars, but also for farming equipment like the tractor. Now tractors do many jobs on the farm, and one of the most important is pulling the plow. The tractor makes plowing much faster, a big advance in farming technology.

Telephones The telephone was created by Alexander Graham Bell in 1875. He was a young inventor who applied new ideas about electromagnets and variations in current. In 1880 telephone service began. The telephone directory was only two pages long! Then telephone wires started going up across the country. To make a call, you spoke into the mouthpiece and told the operator the number of the person you wanted to call. She made the connection. Now we dial the phone number, which signals vast computer networks that connect us. New technology has even made it possible to have cellular telephones or wireless portable phones.

Milk Technology has even changed our food. Long ago, milk was delivered from the farm in large milk cans. It was poured into bottles and then delivered to the front door by milkmen each day. The empty milk bottles were picked up and reused. Now milk is put into easy-to-use cartons and we buy it at the grocery store.